# ★ EQUALITY ★

# EQUALITY

---

## BY LISA MANNETTI

---

*An American Values First Book*
FRANKLIN WATTS 1985
*New York/London/Toronto/Sydney*

Photographs courtesy of:
Bettmann Archive: pp. viii, 7, 9, 19, 21, 26;
UPI/Bettmann Newsphotos: pp. 33, 45, 50;
Sophia Smith Collection: p. 41;
Mimi Forsyth/Monkmeyer Press: p. 53.


Library of Congress Cataloging in Publication Data

Mannetti, Lisa.
Equality.

(An American values first book)
Includes index.
Summary: Examines the origin and historical develop-
ment of equality before the law in America, with an
emphasis on the struggle for equality of Blacks and
other minority groups.
1. Equality before the law—United States—History—
Juvenile literature.  [1. Equality before the law—
History.  2. Civil rights]  I. Title.  II. Series.
KF4764.Z9M36 1985      323.4'0973      85-5405
ISBN 0-531-10039-1

★★★★

# CONTENTS

# ★ EQUALITY ★

Equality was an important ideal to
Thomas Jefferson and other signers of
the Declaration of Independence shown here
—but ensuring equality for all Americans has
been an ongoing struggle since our nation's birth.

# ★ 1 ★

## EQUALITY:
## A CHERISHED
## AMERICAN VALUE

It was 1776. There was a whistling rush of air as the rocket went up and exploded in a glorious burst of color. More fireworks were set off: The smoky night air turned blue, green, gold, red. The loud thunderous booming seemed like cannon fire and nearly drowned out the clanging of the wildly ringing bells. There were bonfires; some of the excited crowd were singing and dancing in the streets. Men and women called out the good news to fellow colonists: The Declaration of Independence had been signed on July Fourth.

Colonial Americans were proud of Thomas Jefferson's words: "All men are created equal." They had faith in and believed in equality as well as the other ideals set forth in the Declaration.

Modern Americans still take pride in the same values, just as they continue to celebrate the Fourth of July. But twentieth-century Americans realize that though the roots of modern ideas about equality stem from colonial times, equality, as it is practiced, has changed considerably in the more than two hundred years since America declared its independence.

# EQUALITY BEFORE THE LAW

The idea that "all men are created equal" does not mean that all people are the same. Some individuals are more intelligent, or more creative, or more talented in a particular area; some may be better athletes or teachers or students. Although people may be "unequal" in skills or accomplishments, they are considered to be equal before the law. Each citizen should receive the same treatment regardless of gender, color, race, religion, or social position.

Equality before the law is based on impartiality. The same law will apply to everyone in the same way. Suppose two children attend the Equal Treatment Academy. One of the rules at the school says no child may play a radio in the classroom. During a math class, both children take out their radios and tune in their favorite stations. The teacher asks both of them to put the radios away. Both children broke a rule by playing their radios, but because the school believes in impartiality and equality before the law, the rule itself determined their treatment—both had to stop playing the radio.

If a government practices equality before the law, its citizens will all be treated the same. For example, if all citizens are entitled to vote, voting rights will apply to all citizens. Or if two people commit the same crime, both will be judged in light of the crime itself, and not according to factors such as wealth, position, or influence.

What happens if equality before the law does not exist?

Suppose two children, Frank and Judy, attend the Governor Whimsy School. At Whimsy, the principal has decided that any child whose last name begins with the letter A will have a higher rank or position than the other children. Children whose last names start with A, therefore, will get special treatment.

A rule at Whimsy states, "Everyone has to eat lunch in the cafeteria." Judy Allen and Frank Baker eat lunch in the gym one day because they want to watch a rehearsal of the school play. The drama teacher sees them.

Both have broken the same rule. But because of Whimsy's policy about last names, the drama teacher believes Frank Baker has committed a more serious offense. Frank and Judy are unequal before the law. Judy Allen receives one demerit for eating lunch in the gym; Frank Baker receives ten. Frank and Judy have broken the same rule, but because they are unequal before the law, the treatment is unequal.

In some periods of history, when people were unequal before the law, the consequences were serious. If two people committed the same crime, one might be severely punished or imprisoned; the other would pay a fine.

## EQUALITY OF OPPORTUNITY

A second kind of equality is equality of opportunity. This type of equality emphasizes the chances or opportunities for citizens to acquire skills they need if they are going to achieve their fullest potential.

Equality of opportunity offers citizens in a democracy the chance to get education, to choose careers, and to better themselves economically.

In the United States, the government has launched policies and passed laws to create an atmosphere of equality of opportunity. Some of these are free public education through grade twelve for all children; programs aimed at creating job opportunities for minorities and women, such as the affirmative action plan, unemployment benefits, and minimum wages.

Today, equality under the law is assured to all American citizens. But Americans have had to struggle long and hard to gain equality. Black Americans held dreams in their hearts for long years to win citizenship and the right to vote. Women, too, crusaded long and hard before they could vote. Women, blacks, and other minority groups battled to achieve the cherished American value—equality.

# ★ 2 ★

## THE ANGLO–AMERICAN
## TRADITION
## OF EQUALITY

The American belief in the value of equality is the outgrowth of a tradition that began in England long before the discovery of the New World. During much of the period historians call the Later Middle Ages (1300–1500), there was a great deal of inequality among people in Europe. Society was divided sharply into different classes. The majority of people had no political, civil, or social rights; and finally, there was no opportunity for most people to get ahead or better themselves economically.

The first or highest class of people were called nobles or aristocrats. This group owned the land and had both power and privileges. The second group were the clergy. Many clergymen, such as bishops, had wealth and influence. Often these high-ranking church officials were the sons of important nobles. Other clergymen were poor parish priests. Their parents were usually from the lower class, and the lives of the priests were frequently as miserable as those of the peasants. The peasants or commoners made up the third and lowest class in medieval society.

*During the Middle Ages most of
the people had no political, civil, or
social rights and lived in complete
servitude to the noble class.*

Life was difficult and often hard for everyone during the Middle Ages. But the life of the noble or lord was far better than the life of the peasant. Peasants, called serfs, toiled on land that belonged to the lord, and performed heavy labor for him. If the lord bought or sold land, the serfs were bought or sold along with the property. The homes of the peasants were small wooden structures plastered over with mud. Food was scarce and often half spoiled. Starvation and disease were common. But the hardest thing for the peasants to bear was the treatment they received from the nobles. Peasants were despised and hated—treated with contempt by the noble class.

The nobles of the Middle Ages had all the political power. The great mass of the people—four-fifths of the population—had no political, civil, or social rights. For example, justice was under the control of the individual nobles. Many of them were unfair and cruel. In fact, many of the laws were unjust as well.

In contrast to modern law, which states that a person accused of a crime is presumed innocent until proven guilty, in the Middle Ages the reverse was true—a person was considered guilty until proven innocent. If one person accused another individual of a crime, stealing, for instance, he was not obligated to prove his charge. The accusation was enough—it was up to the supposed "thief" to prove his innocence. In addition, those who were accused of crimes were often subject to various tortures called ordeals. One ordeal that accused peasants might have to endure was putting a hand into boiling water. If the accused was unharmed during the ordeal, which was unlikely, he was "declared" innocent.

The third factor that contributed to inequality in the Middle Ages was the lack of opportunity for the commoners to get ahead. It was nearly impossible for a peasant to raise himself to the noble class. Merit or hard work or achievement made no difference. In nearly every case, if a person was born a commoner, he remained a commoner.

## THE ENGLISH MAKE
## SOME EARLY PROGRESS
## TOWARD EQUALITY

The cruel king wore a defiant look. His nobles, who had been defiant and rebellious for a long time, had the same defiant air about them. Just the month before, the nobles had banded together and captured the city of London. But the nobles, or barons, had good reason to be rebellious and difficult. John, their king, had been abusing his power for a long time. John was suspected of murdering his nephew, Arthur, a claimant to the English throne. King John had levied high and unfair taxes against the nobles, the Church, and others. He demanded arduous military service that contradicted the code of the times. So, on June 15, 1215, the barons and John met in Runnymede, a meadow in Surrey, England. There the barons forced the reluctant John to sign the famous document known as the Magna Charta or Great Charter.

Despite the many injustices that existed during the Middle Ages, the Magna Charta represented a step toward the

*King John signing the Magna Charta
in 1215, a beginning step
toward a more just society*

★ 8 ★

beginnings of egalitarianism, that is, the belief and practice of political and social equality. Although the document was really a contract between the king and his barons, the Magna Charta was important to future generations for several reasons. It limited the power of the king and prevented him from levying arbitrary taxes without the consent of the common council in England. The charter also did away with many legal injustices, such as condemning a person on the basis of rumor or suspicion. Instead, all free men were entitled to a trial by a jury of their peers, or equals in rank, if they were accused of a crime. Finally, among other provisions, the charter permitted the nobles to elect twenty-five members of their group to insure that the king kept his word.

Other steps toward equality were gradually made. In England, serfdom disappeared. Towns and cities grew, and as a result a new middle class began to emerge. The members of this new middle class were able to acquire money and political influence. In addition, a group was formed that is the basis of today's English Parliament. Toward the end of the thirteenth century, a man named Simon de Montfort, who was the brother-in-law of King Henry III, called an assembly or Parliament. In addition to the nobles, Simon asked two knights from each shire, or county, and two citizens from each of the twenty-one most important towns. By the end of the medieval period, Parliament had the authority to limit the power of the king, to regulate taxes, and to assist in the law-making process.

## THE GLORIOUS REVOLUTION

England was slowly making advances toward equality. The Magna Charta and the formation of Parliament helped pave the way. Many American ideas of democracy and equality were born in England during this time. One event that especially influenced the growth of English and American democracy was the Glorious Revolution of 1688–1689.

At the time, James II, a Catholic, was the king of England. He tried to establish Catholicism as the official religion of the country. People were fearful that if he succeeded, England would be dominated by the pope, the head of the Catholic Church. They wanted a Protestant monarch who would not have religious ties to Rome. James's daughter, Mary, was a Protestant. She was married to William of Orange, the ruler of the Netherlands. William was a Protestant, too.

A group of seven important Englishmen secretly invited Prince William and Princess Mary to come to England and accept the throne. When William arrived from Holland with his army, he marched to London and occupied the city without a single battle. James was deserted by his supporters and even by his soldiers. He fled to France. William and Mary became the joint rulers of England.

The results of this "bloodless" revolution were far reaching. New freedoms and rights were granted to the English when William and Mary agreed to the Bill of Rights, which Parliament passed into law on December 16, 1689. Among other things, the bill prevented the king from suspending laws or inflicting cruel punishments and prevented him from levying taxes without the consent of Parliament. In addition, the English won the right to petition the government, and Parliament established freedom of speech and freedom of the press. Parliament also passed the Toleration Act, which granted religious freedom to many Christians who had not been allowed to worship as they chose.

England's Glorious Revolution and the new freedoms and rights that came about inspired other people around the world. Many agreed with the idea that a king should not be an absolute monarch. The English system showed that a limited government was a good idea. One person who was influenced by these ideas was Thomas Jefferson, the author of the Declaration of Independence. The founders of our country were also influenced by this tradition; much of the English Bill of Rights was included in the first ten amendments to the American Constitution.

## THE AMERICAN WAY

After the signing of the Magna Charta, and the Glorious Revolution, the English were making strides toward equality. And although our democratic ideals are rooted in the English system, America—even in its colonial days—provided more equality for its people than England.

One factor in American colonial life that contributed to much greater equality was the lack of a rigid class system. There were social divisions in America—wealthy landowners had a higher social position than shopkeepers, artisans, laborers, and the like. But even a servant could aspire to the highest social position through hard work and achievement. Even in colonial days, America was a land of opportunity.

Another factor that helped the growth of American equality was the spread of religious tolerance. Some early colonists who came to America were fleeing religious persecution in their native lands. At first, many of these colonists—although they sought religious freedom for their own religious groups or sects—did not tolerate others. A person who practiced a different faith might not be permitted to vote or hold public office. Sometimes those of different faiths were punished in harsher ways. Anne Hutchinson, for example, had deeply religious views, but they conflicted with those of the Puritans. She was tried by a court in 1637 and banished from the colony of Massachusetts. As time went on, however, the idea of religious tolerance gained ground, and more and more people were able to take part in the democratic process.

## EARLY EQUALITY
## AND ITS LIMITS

When Jefferson wrote the Declaration of Independence, he was stating the fundamentals of democracy: "We hold these truths to be self-evident: that all men are created equal, that they are endowed by their Creator with certain unalienable rights, that among these are life, liberty, and the pursuit of happiness." The rights Jefferson termed "unalienable"—life, liberty, and the pursuit of happiness—are rights that no government has the power to take away from its people. They belong to all people by virtue of their humanity.

When the founding fathers wrote the Constitution, they guaranteed Americans a number of important rights and freedoms, including the right to a speedy trial and to be represented by a lawyer. They ensured that Americans had such civil liberties as freedom of religion, freedom of the press, freedom of speech, and the freedom to assemble and petition the government.

Jefferson's vision—that all men are created equal—was only an ideal at the time. At the time of its birth, the American government was very liberal in comparison to other governments, but equality was limited.

Black slaves were considered the property of their owners, and even free blacks were restricted in their rights. Women, too, had very few rights in the early days of America. They could not vote; married women had no right to own property. Some other groups whose numbers placed them in a minority in the population were without rights, as well. Each of these groups—blacks, women, and minorities—had to fight for equality. The history of their struggles is the history of attempts to make a reality of Jefferson's ideal that all men—indeed all people—are equal.

# ★ 3 ★

## THE BLACK EXPERIENCE: SLAVERY

In 1619, the first blacks brought to Jamestown, Virginia, were indentured servants. They were to serve their masters for a certain number of years and then be set free. But as time went on, all blacks brought here were made slaves.

Black men, women, and children were captured in their native Africa. They were forced to wear chains and collars and to endure a long and dangerous sea voyage to America. Many of them died from diseases and the terrible conditions on board ship. Some committed suicide from despair.

After the terrors of the voyage, more horrors awaited them. They were denied their freedom, their cultural heritage, their humanity: Blacks were sold for profit as slaves. They were "property," owned by the white men who bought them.

### COLONIAL SLAVERY

By 1765, there were between 300,000 and 400,000 blacks in colonial America. Some blacks had gained their freedom. For example, those whose ancestors had been indentured servants, or whose mothers were white, were considered free. Some blacks had been able to save money and purchase their freedom; others had been set free by their former masters. But most blacks were slaves. And, whether they were free or held in slavery, blacks were regarded as inferior by white colonists.

In the North, slaves were often the servants of wealthy families. Some slaves were craftsmen, such as blacksmiths or carpenters. In the colonies of the agricultural South, owners depended more heavily on slaves to work in the fields. They used more slaves to help farm their large tobacco, rice, or indigo plantations, than did Northerners who tended to have smaller farms. As a result, there were many more slaves in the South than in the North.

## CONSTITUTIONAL COMPROMISES AND SLAVERY

During the hot summer of 1787, when the delegates were meeting in Philadelphia for the Constitutional Convention, Northerners and Southerners were divided in their opinions about the counting of slaves. Since representation in the House of Representatives is based on population, Southerners, who had many slaves, wanted to include all the slaves in the population count. But when it came to taxes, Southerners did not want the slaves counted. The Northern delegates were in favor of the reverse. They wanted to count the slaves for the purpose of taxes but not for representation. Northerners feared if the Southerners had their own way, Southerners would pay too little in taxes and have too many votes in Congress. In the end, a compromise, or agreement, was reached known as the Three-Fifths Compromise. The delegates decided three-fifths of each state's slave population would be counted to determine both the amount of taxes to be paid and the number of representatives in Congress from each state.

Another conflict between the Northern and Southern delegates arose over importing slaves from other countries. Finally, after a long debate, the Slave Trade Compromise was reached. In this agreement, the delegates decided slaves could be imported until 1808—that is, about twenty years after the Constitution was adopted. After that time, Congress would decide what to do about importing slaves. Some people believed that slavery would gradually come to an end. But long before 1808, slavery expanded more rapidly than anyone could have imagined.

## KING COTTON

In 1793, a clever young man named Eli Whitney invented a machine called the cotton gin. Before the cotton gin came into use, processing cotton—cleaning and separating the seeds from the fibrous bolls of cotton—was a tedious and difficult job that had to be done by hand. A slave who worked hard at it all day could remove the seeds from only a few pounds of cotton. But the cotton gin could process hundreds of pounds in a single day.

Whitney's machine used a system of revolving rollers or cylinders set next to each other. One cylinder was set with many saw teeth. When the cylinder was turned, the teeth pulled the raw cotton through a comblike grid that had closely spaced ribs. The cotton fibers could pass through the comb, but the seeds were too big and fell into a space below the cylinders. The second, smaller, roller had brushes attached to it that collected the cleaned or "ginned" cotton.

Whitney's cotton gin made cotton an extremely valuable crop in the South. In 1790, before the use of his invention, only 4,000 bales of cotton were produced each year. The number rose higher and higher, and by 1860, the number of bales jumped to 4 million.

The cotton industry allowed many Southerners to become extremely wealthy in a short time. One reason was the rapidly growing demand for cotton. The crop affected so many people worldwide who clamored for cotton that Southerners would often say that cotton was "king."

Many plantation owners believed that slavery was necessary in order to continue to produce cotton. They depended on the slaves to plant, pick, and gin cotton. To meet the demand for cotton, more and more slaves were brought here. By 1860, there were approximately 4 million slaves in the South. Whitney's labor-saving device bound the coils of slavery and servitude more tightly.


## SLAVE LIFE

Slaves performed many types of jobs. Some learned trades; they were carpenters or bricklayers or wheelwrights. Many were taught household duties. They served as butlers, cooks, seamstresses, nurses. Both men and women worked in the fields. Most worked from before sunrise until after sunset. Their work day was long and hard. Slaves did not receive any wages for their labors.

Slaves were given clothes and shoes and some food by their owners, but they were expected to provide some for themselves. Some slaves planted their own small gardens or kept a few hogs or chickens near their quarters for this purpose. They tended to their own small gardening or farming

*A slave auction in
pre-Civil War Virginia*

chores after they had completed the day's work for their owner.

Some slaves were treated very harshly by their owners or the overseers who supervised their work. Slaves could be whipped, branded, or maimed. Families were sometimes separated if the owner sold one member of the family to a different owner.

The laws governing slaves were strict, as well. Slaves could not leave the plantation without permission. At night, they were expected to stay in their houses. Slaves were also taught never to answer back to any white person, or to strike back even in self-defense.

In addition to the slaves, there were about 250,000 free blacks. Laws concerning free blacks were severe. Blacks had to carry passes to prove they were not slaves. They were not permitted to assemble for any purpose—often they could not even gather in churches unless a white person was present. Some laws even prevented their learning to read and write. Free blacks paid property taxes, but they were not permitted to vote. They were not equal to whites before the law.

## THE ABOLITIONISTS

From colonial times onward, some Americans believed slavery was wrong. Those who condemned it and tried to bring an end to slavery were called abolitionists. Between 1820 and 1860, the antislavery movement grew stronger. By the

*Abolitionists circulated newspapers and pamphlets like the* Emancipator *to make people realize the horrors and injustices of slavery.*

# EMANCIPATOR—*EXTRA.*

NEW-YORK, SEPTEMBER 2, 1839.

## American Anti-Slavery Almanac for 1840.

The seven cuts following, are selected from thirteen, which may be found in the Anti-Slavery Almanac for 1840. They represent well-authenticated facts, and illustrate in various ways, the cruelties daily inflicted upon three millions of native born Americans, by their fellow-countrymen! A brief explanation follows each cut.

*The peculiar "Domestic Institutions of our Southern brethren."*

*Selling a Mother from her Child.*

*Mothers with young Children at work in the field.*

*A Woman chained to a Girl, and a Man in irons at work in the field.*

*"They can't take care of themselves"; explained in an interesting article.*

*Hunting Slaves with dogs and guns. A Slave drowned by the logs.*

*Servility of the Northern States in arresting and returning fugitive Slaves.*

middle of the 1830s, about 150,000 Americans belonged to groups and societies that were formed in the hope of abolishing slavery.

Abolitionists circulated pamphlets and petitions calling for an end to slavery in America. In addition, former slaves lectured against the evils of slavery. One was Frederick Douglass, who described the cruelty and beatings he had endured as a slave. He was one of the best-known orators of his day, and his brilliant speeches helped further the cause of the abolitionists. Douglass campaigned for equal rights for blacks throughout his lifetime.

Some abolitionists were more militant or aggressive in their efforts. In 1829 David Walker, a young free black, published an essay titled "Appeal." Walker believed any means, including force, should be used by blacks to gain freedom. Another aggressive abolitionist was William Lloyd Garrison. Garrison, a white, was so outspoken against slavery he angered Americans all over the country. Once, in Baltimore, a slave trader sued him; when Garrison couldn't pay the fine, he was put in jail. On another occasion, the state of Georgia offered a $5,000 reward for his arrest. In 1831, Garrison published a newspaper in Boston called the *Liberator* which championed immediate and complete freedom for slaves.

Some abolitionists helped organize what was known as the Underground Railroad. Both black and white Americans, called "conductors," aided fugitive slaves to hide by day and travel by night until they reached the next "station" or house. It was a long and dangerous journey, because the escaped slaves were considered outlaws until they reached Canada. One of the most famous fugitive slaves, Harriet Tubman, returned to the South often and conducted many others northward to freedom. She was called the "Moses of Her People."

# ★ 4 ★

## THE BLACK EXPERIENCE:
## THE CIVIL WAR
## AND RECONSTRUCTION

In 1860, a tall gaunt man was elected to the presidency. Two years before, in 1858, Abraham Lincoln had declared the United States could not remain "half slave and half free."

Lincoln hated slavery, but he was not an abolitionist. His chief goal was to preserve the Union. He wrote: "If I could save the Union without freeing *any* slave, I would do it; if I could save it by freeing *all* the slaves, I would do it; and if I could do it by freeing some and leaving others alone, I would also do that."

When the news came that Lincoln had been elected, South Carolina seceded from the Union. Soon Texas, Louisiana, Mississippi, Florida, Georgia, and Alabama withdrew as well. A month before Lincoln's inauguration in March, 1861, delegates from the seceded states met and established the Confederate States of America. They chose Jefferson Davis as president.

Then on April 12, 1861, Confederate troops attacked Fort Sumter in Charleston, South Carolina. The war was on. The outbreak of hostilities drove the border states of Virginia, North Carolina, Tennessee, and Arkansas to the side of the Confederacy.

# THE CIVIL WAR
## 1861–1865

As the fighting continued over the next few years, more and more Northerners began to believe they had to win the war, not only to preserve the Union, as Lincoln originally declared, but to abolish slavery. Then, on January 1, 1863, Lincoln issued the Emancipation Proclamation, which stated "All persons held as slaves within any state or part of a state in rebellion against the United States, shall be then, thenceforward and forever free." The proclamation aroused great fervor among Northerners, and helped spur them on to victory.

Though the Emancipation Proclamation was important, it did not end slavery altogether in the United States. Slaves in border states, and in some parts of Virginia and Louisiana which were already held by Union troops were not freed. The 13th Amendment ratified eight months after the end of the war, ended slavery throughout the United States and its territories.


## RECONSTRUCTION

When the war was over, 200,000 men had died in battle or from wounds, 413,000 were dead from diseases or accidents. The South lay in ruins: Cities were reduced to rubble, bridges, roads, crops, fields, and railroads had been destroyed; many graceful homes had been set afire—nothing remained but ash heaps in broken, blackened foundations. Many Southerners, blacks and whites, were homeless and hungry.

The period following the Civil War is known as the

Reconstruction era. It was a time of restoring the Union. Congress enacted many new laws, some of which were considered radical.

Lincoln's view about restoring the Union was expressed when he stated, "With malice toward none, with charity for all." But he did not live to see his reconstruction program carried out. He was assassinated while watching a play at Ford's Theatre on April 14, 1865, by John Wilkes Booth, an actor.

In 1865, Congress created the Freedman's Bureau to help former slaves if they needed food, clothing, or medical attention. Schools were established to teach blacks to read and write. Many Southerners believed members of the bureau were encouraging blacks to resent their former masters. Then, in the summer and fall of 1865, the situation was aggravated when a rumor was started that every former slave would get "forty acres and a mule" from the government for a Christmas present. Many blacks believed the rumor. The truth was that land where taxes were owed, or land that had been abandoned by owners, could be distributed to the former slaves in parcels no larger than forty acres. But in the end, most of the 800,000 acres the bureau controlled were given back to the former owners. Many blacks who hoped to own their own farms were disappointed; many Southern whites felt the bureau had encouraged those false hopes and they were angry.

Some Southerners were bitter toward their former slaves. They could not adjust to the idea of freedom for blacks. As a result, Southern lawmakers began to create laws known as Black Codes. The codes were based on the old slave codes that had existed before the war. In many Southern states, blacks were denied their civil rights. Blacks could not travel without permits; they could not carry firearms, or assemble unless a white person was present. After dark, blacks were forbidden to be out in the streets. In most states, because white Southerners wanted economic superiority, the Black Codes spelled out strict labor contracts and prohibited blacks from starting businesses. Blacks were free, but they were very much unequal to whites.

Many Congressmen were angered by the Black Codes. They sincerely wanted to help the freed slaves. Other Congressmen were not so high-minded. But, both these radical groups banded together and introduced reconstructionist legislation in Congress. One outcome was the 14th Amendment, passed in 1868, which granted citizenship to former slaves. Then, in 1870, the 15th Amendment gave the franchise, or the right to vote, to blacks. Both amendments gave important rights to blacks. As citizens they were entitled to equal protection under the laws. As voters they were able to participate in the democratic process.

After the passage of the 15th Amendment, for the first time in the South blacks registered and voted. Many took advantage of their new right, and blacks ran for, and were elected to office in every state in the South. During the Reconstruction era, twenty-two blacks served in Congress, as well.

In the meantime, angry white Southerners banded together in secret societies such as the Knights of the White Camellia and the Ku Klux Klan (KKK). The goal of these groups was to terrorize blacks and prevent them from voting, holding public office, and practicing their political rights. At night, members of the Klan, dressed in white robes and pointed hoods, tried to frighten blacks with threats or by burning wooden crosses near their homes. Klansmen often brutalized blacks by beating or lynching them.

*This drawing by Frank Bellow is titled*
*"Visit of the Ku Klux Klan." After the*
*Civil War, many white Southerners formed groups*
*like the KKK whose purpose was to terrorize*
*blacks and keep them from exercising their*
*newly granted political rights.*

In addition to violence and scare tactics, such as the KKK practiced to prevent blacks from pursuing equality, some Southern states began passing laws to deny blacks their rights. Two examples of this were the poll tax and the literacy test.

The poll tax was a tax that had to be paid by every voter; the literacy test was given to see if a voter could read or write. Since many Southern blacks had never been educated, and did not have enough money to pay the tax, they were prevented from voting.

Beginning with Tennessee in 1881, most Southern states began to pass Jim Crow laws. According to these laws, blacks and whites had to ride in separate rail cars. Soon segregation—the separation of races—included schools, streetcars, railroad stations, parks, playgrounds, and other public places.

Blacks were angered and hurt by the Jim Crow laws. They felt as if they weren't "good enough" to mingle with whites. Some blacks who were fair-skinned enough to "pass" for white moved north or to other areas where local people didn't know them, because many whites considered a person black if he or she had black ancestors, no matter how fair-skinned they appeared.

In 1892, a man named Plessy took a seat in a train reserved for whites in Louisiana. Plessy was one-eighth black and seven-eighths white, but the conductor insisted he sit in the car for blacks. When Plessy refused, he was arrested and convicted of violating the Jim Crow law. He appealed his case to the Supreme Court. But Plessy lost his case, and in 1896, the Supreme Court ruled it was legal to provide "separate but equal" facilities for blacks and whites. The Supreme Court's decision held for the next half century.

# ★ 5 ★

## BLACKS STRUGGLE
## FOR EQUALITY

Segregation and discrimination. Up until twenty years ago, those words formed the pattern in the lives of black Americans. But what do the words mean? What was it like to face segregation and discrimination?

Imagine that you were a black child in a public place on a hot day, and very thirsty. A sign would have informed you that there were two water fountains—one for "whites," a second for "coloreds." Perhaps you might be nearer the fountain that was for white people, or there was no one drinking from it, while at the other there was a long line—none of that would have mattered. You would be permitted to drink only from the one designated for "coloreds." That is segregation—the separating of races. But in the United States, it wasn't merely a matter of water fountains. Jim Crow laws required blacks to use separate public bathrooms, separate entrances and exits in buildings, and separate schools, elevators, restaurants, and cemeteries.

Discrimination—making distinctions among people, treating them differently because of prejudice—had a profound impact on blacks as well.

Imagine that you had studied very hard to become a lawyer. As a professional, you would have made your parents and friends justifiably proud of you. You may have been one of the few lucky enough to get a good job and diligently save money. Imagine that you had selected a nice house in a good neighborhood, had acquired the money for the down payment, and earned enough to pay the mortgage. Because you were black, you would not, in all probability, have been allowed to purchase the house. You might have been told a lie—that it had just been sold, perhaps for more money than you offered, or you may have been bluntly informed, "We don't sell to your kind. We don't want your kind in this neighborhood."

In the United States, blacks faced discrimination in schools, at jobs, in housing, and in many other areas. American blacks led lives of frustration, of denied opportunities, of hurt and anger and pain because of their skin color— because of segregation and discrimination.

The fight to end segregation and discrimination was a long and difficult one for black Americans. For one thing, segregation was legal after the "separate but equal" notion the Court had ruled on in the Plessy case in 1896. But legal segregation created many problems. Because blacks and whites were separated, people developed psychological barriers—fears, prejudices, and misunderstandings. In addition, although the facilities for blacks were supposed to be equal, they were not. In most cases, black schools, parks, rest rooms, elevators, and other facilities were vastly inferior to those used by whites.

Segregation contributed to inequality among blacks and whites and caused many problems. One of these was segregated schools. Schools for blacks often had smaller budgets than schools for whites. There were fewer textbooks, and they were older. Equipment, teaching aids, and sports programs were not of the same quality as those in schools for whites. Teacher's salaries were lower. These poorer schools were turning out badly educated children. In effect, black children did not have an equal opportunity to be educated.

Then, in 1954, in a landmark case called *Brown* v. *the Board of Education of Topeka,* the Supreme Court unanimously rejected the old "separate but equal" notion and ruled that segregation was illegal. But reform was slow.

In some areas, violent conflicts arose when integration, or desegregation as it was called, was attempted. In 1957, the governor of Arkansas called out the National Guard to keep black students out of Central High School in Little Rock. The first black girl who tried to enter was named Elizabeth Eckford. Elizabeth, dressed in her new checked skirt, was excited and anxious about her first day at Central. But when she got there, a crowd called her names. Then a National Guardsman raised his bayonet so she could not pass by him and enter the school. The crowd was shouting at Elizabeth; one woman spat on her. Discouraged, Elizabeth boarded a bus and left the scene at the school. Eventually, President Dwight D. Eisenhower ordered the National Guard to uphold the Supreme Court ruling and protect black students who wished to attend Central.

## THE CIVIL RIGHTS MOVEMENT

After segregation in schools had been outlawed, blacks began to mobilize for equality and civil rights more vigorously. One of the most famous efforts to obtain black rights was the Montgomery, Alabama, bus boycott.

On December 1, 1955, a forty-year-old black seamstress

named Rosa Parks took a bus on her way home from work. She sat down in the front section of the bus—in the section reserved for white passengers. The driver told her to change her seat. Mrs. Parks refused. She was arrested for violating the law.

Members of the black community heard the news of Mrs. Parks' arrest. Under the leadership of Dr. Martin Luther King, Jr., thousands of blacks joined in a protest and boycotted the Montgomery bus system. Dr. King and the other leaders of the boycott were arrested. But the boycott was successful: Ten months after Rosa Parks refused to sit in the black section of the bus, the Supreme Court ruled the segregation law in Alabama was unconstitutional.

Dr. Martin Luther King, Jr. was born in Atlanta. At age 15 he entered college and later studied to become a minister. In 1956, Dr. King was elected president of the Southern Christian Leadership Conference.

Throughout his career, Dr. King advocated nonviolence. He believed peaceful solutions could be found to settle the problems of racial issues and to further the cause of equal rights for blacks.

One of the most successful demonstrations for black rights was the march on Washington, D.C., in August 1963. More than 250,000 blacks and whites arrived by trains, cars, planes, and buses to meet in the capital. The group marched from the Washington Monument to the Lincoln Memorial; many carried signs to show their support for equal rights. At

*Martin Luther King, Jr., giving his dramatic "I Have a Dream" speech at the Washington Mall in 1963*

the Memorial, famous actors, folk singers, and writers rallied the crowd with civil rights songs and speeches. The climax was Martin Luther King's dramatic and moving "I Have a Dream" speech. Dr. King believed that freedom, justice, and understanding among races were all possible. He said, "I have a dream that one day this nation will rise up and live out the true meaning of its creed: 'that all men are created equal.'"

In April 1968, Dr. King went to Memphis, Tennessee, to lead striking sanitation workers on a peaceful protest march. On April 4, as he stood outside on the second-floor landing of his motel, talking with friends, he was assassinated.

King was moderate in his views on civil rights. Many activists agreed with his perspective and participated in freedom rides, freedom marches, and nonviolent demonstrations. The activists used sit-ins in efforts to end discrimination in restaurants, movie theaters, libraries, and other public places.

In contrast, some black leaders were more militant and aggressive. The Black Panther Party, for example, advocated the use of violence, if necessary, to achieve their goals. Another extremist was Malcolm X. While the moderates, like Dr. King, believed integration was possible, Malcolm X disagreed. He felt blacks and whites had to live separately, apart from one another. Later, Malcolm X concluded that the segregation he preached was not a solution to civil rights problems.

## ACHIEVEMENTS OF THE CIVIL RIGHTS MOVEMENT

The civil rights movement brought changes to American life. First, more people became aware of the injustices and inequalities that existed in the United States. Blacks and whites realized there was a need for new laws that would end segregation and discrimination.

In 1964, Congress passed the Civil Rights Act, which declared segregation in public places illegal. Blacks were allowed to enter libraries, hotels, parks, restaurants, and other public places they had been barred from. In addition, the act outlawed job discrimination. The illegality of job discrimination was an important gain in the struggle for equal rights, because blacks had often been denied jobs, promotions, raises, and bonuses that white workers received.

A year later, Congress approved the Voting Rights Act of 1965. Federal supervisors went to certain districts to see that blacks were given equal opportunity to register to vote. The Voting Rights Act was important because throughout the South, many blacks had been prevented from voting. Methods used by white officials were similar to those used to prevent blacks from registering and voting during the Reconstruction era. When blacks tried to register, white officials would give them tests to measure literacy or knowledge of government. These tests were not given to whites who wished to register. Sometimes registration officials rejected applications blacks filled out if the individual made any errors or left any spaces blank. But if a white person made mistakes filling out the form, they accepted the application without question.

As a result of the Voting Rights Act, more blacks were able to register to vote. As time went on, the numbers of blacks elected to public office began to rise. Blacks were elected to the Senate and to the House of Representatives. By 1980, several major cities, including Washington, D.C., Los Angeles, Atlanta, and Detroit had black mayors. More recently, the Reverend Jesse Jackson sought the Democratic

Party nomination for president in 1984. Although the Reverend Jackson was not nominated, his campaign represented a landmark in American history, and many people believe he has paved the way for a black president in the future.

The struggle for blacks to gain full equality has been a long one, and one that is not finished, even today. From the Civil War onward, gains have been made, lost, and won again. Attitudes, opinions, and prejudices have changed over the years, but slowly. Nevertheless, laws are helping blacks gain equal rights.

# ★ 6 ★

## WOMEN STRUGGLE
## FOR EQUALITY

When the founders wrote the Constitution, they were concerned with the rights of Americans. But the Constitution did not provide all people with equality. Blacks, for example, have had to fight for their rights. Another group the founders left out are women. They, too, have had to struggle long and hard for equality.

Women were thought to be inferior to men—less intelligent, less capable, and weaker. As a result, laws and lifestyles reflected that attitude. Women had few legal rights. They could not vote. Women's opportunities for jobs and education were almost nonexistent. They were not equal with men.

Most men and women believed a woman's place was at home taking care of her family and her house. Many people felt it was unladylike or improper for a woman to work. In order to train girls in the tasks of a housewife, they were taught cooking, sewing, needlework, and other domestic skills. They were not allowed to train for any other occupation.

# BEGINNINGS OF
# FEMINISM

Some women did not believe that all women were inferior to men. They thought that given the opportunity, most women would be able to accomplish a great deal and make important contributions to society. One of these women was Lucretia Coffin Mott, who was born in Massachusetts in 1793. Lucretia was a Quaker who championed many causes. In 1833, she helped organize an abolitionist group called the American Anti-Slavery Society. Her home was a station on the Underground Railroad.

Another early feminist was Elizabeth Cady Stanton, born in Johnstown, New York, in 1815. She and Lucretia Mott met, and in 1840 they went to England to attend an international convention to abolish slavery. The American women wanted to take an active part in the convention. This caused a furor among the delegates. For days, the conventioneers argued back and forth about equal rights for women and whether the women should be allowed to participate. In the end, Mott and Stanton were required to sit behind a curtain, where they could not be seen. They were not permitted to speak at the convention or present their views and opinions on slavery.

Lucretia and Elizabeth began to realize there was a need for a women's rights movement. So, in July, 1848, they organized the first women's rights convention in Seneca Falls, New York. More than 100 delegates attended the convention; some were men who believed in the women's cause.

The convention adopted a declaration that firmly stated the foundation of its ideals. It read, "We hold these truths to be self-evident: That all men and women are created equal." The declaration called for women's right to equal opportunities for jobs, in professions, trades, and businesses; for women's right to equality before the law; and for women's right to vote. Although many of these demands were not met for years, the convention laid the foundation for the women's movement.

Another early advocate of equality for women was Sojourner Truth. She was born a slave in Ulster County, New York, under the name of Isabella Baumfree. When a New York law in 1828 banned slavery, Isabella was set free.

Later she changed her name to Sojourner Truth to indicate that she was on a journey to spread the message of truth, freedom, and equality. She became one of the best-known abolitionists, and was the first black woman to speak out against slavery. Sojourner believed strongly in women's rights as well. At meetings when men argued that women were inferior, Sojourner described her days in the field to prove women could work as well as men and deserved political and social equality.

## ISSUES AND RIGHTS

The feminists of the nineteenth century knew that in order for women to be equal with men, changes in attitudes and opinions were necessary. Women needed economic and political power to gain their rights. Feminists sought reform in the areas of property rights, the rights of workers, and most importantly, the vote.

During much of the 1800s, married women had no legal

rights to their property—control was automatically passed to their husbands. For example, suppose a businessman owned a building in town and wanted to leave the property to his daughter as an inheritance. If she were married, her husband would have legal control of the building. And without his consent, she, in turn, would not be able to make a will and leave property to the person of her choice. In addition, a woman's wages belonged to her husband; married women could not bring lawsuits in their own names or make contracts. Without property rights, women could not be independent; they were not equal to men.

Women of the nineteenth century tried to improve rights for workers. One problem they encountered was the low wages paid for long working hours. Some women spent sixty-two hours a week in factories, making shoes or hats or sewing dresses; at the end of that time they brought home a paycheck of about $2.16. Another problem feminists wanted to eliminate was unsafe working conditions. Accidents were common occurrences. Women who sewed the same kinds of pieces over and over again all day long sometimes became distracted, or had trouble seeing in poorly lighted workrooms, or became tired. When that happened, they often accidentally let the heavy sewing machine needles run over their hands. Women crusaded and protested to get shorter hours, better wages, and safer conditions.

The women who tried to gain suffrage—the right to vote—were known as suffragists. One of the best known was Susan B. Anthony, who was born in Massachusetts in 1820. She devoted herself untiringly to the women's movement. When the 15th Amendment, which gave the vote to blacks, was proposed, Susan B. Anthony and her friend Elizabeth Cady Stanton wanted women included as well. But

*A suffrage parade in*
*New York City in 1913*

many people believed if voting for women was included, the amendment would not be ratified, and the ex-slaves would lose the chance to win voting rights.

Susan B. Anthony did not give up. She chose to interpret the amendment as though it applied to women. In 1872, she persuaded election inspectors in Rochester, N.Y., to allow her to register and vote, along with twelve of her women friends. Anthony was arrested, fined, and eventually released. Although accounts of her highly publicized trial aroused sympathy for the women's movement, it was still many years before American women were permitted to vote.

The suffragist movement inspired mixed points of view in both men and women. Some men agreed women should be allowed to vote; one of these was William Lloyd Garrison, the famous abolitionist. But many citizens and most newspapers ridiculed early feminist efforts. Outspoken suffragists were branded in the press as "The Shrieking Sisterhood." Meetings and demonstrations were broken up, and the crusading women were exposed to taunts, jeers, and threats that bordered on violence.

The suffragists kept working toward their goal. Wyoming became the first state to give women the power to vote. The people felt so strongly about this issue that in 1899, when Wyoming was applying for statehood, Wyoming declared, "we will remain out of the Union a hundred years rather than come in without women's suffrage." Slowly but surely, the feminists inched toward their goal. In 1900, women voted in four states. In 1916, the total was twelve. Finally, in 1919, Congress approved the 19th Amendment to the Constitution which gave the franchise to women. It became law on August 26, 1920.

# THE ERA

The Equal Rights Amendment (ERA), first proposed to Congress in 1923, simply states, "Equality of Rights under the law shall not be abridged by the United States or by any state on account of sex." But the ERA has had a stormy history, and the controversy that surrounds the amendment has not yet been resolved.

Supporters of the ERA believe it is a necessary step to insure full equality for women under the law. Opponents of the amendment argue the ERA might cause a breakdown in the traditional bonds of the family in America. Some women fear that with the passage of an equal-rights amendment, women may be drafted into the military, or that women might lose alimony payments in divorce cases.

Over the years, many women's groups continued to seek support for the ERA. In March, 1972, forty-nine years after the amendment was originally proposed, Congress approved it. Supporters of the bill were enthusiastic; they were sure the states would ratify it quickly, making the ERA the 27th Amendment to the Constitution.

In 1973, thirty of the required thirty-eight states needed to approve the ERA had done so. Then the number of states rose to thirty-five by 1978. As the deadline for ratification— March 22, 1979—drew near, supporters were worried. But Congress granted a three-year extension until June 30, 1982. Still, no new states ratified the amendment, and the ERA was defeated.

In the absence of a national ERA, some states are considering including equal-rights amendments in their own state constitutions. For example, in 1985, New York's legislature will make consideration of a state ERA a top priority.

One reason people feel the Equal Rights Amendment to the Constitution is needed is to assure women full equality with men, including equal pay for equal jobs. Women have traditionally been paid much less than men for jobs, and, in fact, earn only fifty-nine cents for every dollar men are paid.

## COUNTERING DISCRIMINATION

Many women's groups, including the National Organization for Women (NOW), which was founded in 1966, are dedicated to eliminating discrimination.

Women have successfully fought discrimination by filing lawsuits against companies and universities that kept women subservient in the work force through unequal hiring, enrolling, and promoting practices. Great strides have been made, and women have pursued successful careers as professors, lawyers, doctors, and athletes. Women have been able to enter other fields long dominated by men as well. Woman are now carpenters, construction workers, and plumbers. They work as police officers and have careers in government and the military. In 1984, when Democratic presidential candidate Walter Mondale selected Representative Geraldine Ferraro, the first woman to seek the vice presidency, as his running mate, many people considered the landmark a true breakthrough for women.

Women have also tried to change society's attitude toward them. They have discouraged the use of words and phrases that exclude or devalue women, such as the practice of referring to women, even those who have clearly reached adulthood, as "girls." Since men were never called "boys,"

*As the Democratic vice-presidential candidate in 1984, Geraldine Ferraro symbolized the great strides women have made in gaining equality.*

women felt the use of the term "girls" was inappropriate and demeaning.

Women have tried to eliminate masculine and feminine stereotypes in books, films, and on television. They felt that by portraying certain jobs, attitudes, and emotions as exclusively male or female, both men and women developed limited expectations. Several years ago, a scenario might have showed a pretty young mother, wearing a dress and apron, baking cookies. Her son would be in the other room playing with his trucks and her daughter holding a doll. The family would be awaiting the arrival of the father. As more women moved into the work force, media images of their roles changed. Women and men and their children are now portrayed in a much expanded way. Feminists believe these new portraits are much more accurate and beneficial to men and women alike.

From the struggles of the early feminists onward, the efforts of women to gain full equality in areas such as property rights, voting, and overcoming discrimination have all ultimately been directed toward one goal. Their aim has been, and continues to be, to seek improvements for all society by assuring that every person can fulfill his or her potential.

# ★ 7 ★

## OTHER GROUPS
## DEMAND RIGHTS

As a nation, America has taken steps to assure its citizens equality before the law. But in some important ways, inequality still exists for many minority groups. Encouraged by the achievements of the civil-rights and women's movements, most minority groups, including Hispanics, American Indians, the handicapped, and the elderly, have been demanding their rights, too.

The Hispanics—immigrants from and descendents of those born in Mexico, Cuba, Central and South America, and Puerto Rico—numbered approximately fifteen million in 1980. They are the second-largest minority group in America. They are a diverse people, but have a common Spanish heritage.

Many Hispanics have faced discrimination in employment, education, and housing. Since many Hispanics cannot speak English, they encounter worse discrimination.

Suppose your family decided to move to another country and you didn't know the language. Movies, television, ads, and books would be a meaningless jumble of words—you might catch some of the meaning and ideas from the pictures. But at school you'd probably have a hard time understanding your teacher, making friends, and expressing your ideas.

In the evening, you'd feel better and more confident when you returned to your family. You wouldn't have to hesitate to think of the right word, in a strange and difficult language, for what you wanted to say. You would understand every word your parents said, and you wouldn't feel foolish or left out because you couldn't understand what was being said around you.

Many Hispanic children and adults faced these problems when they came to the United States. Children had trouble learning in school; their parents had difficulties getting housing and jobs.

Beginning in the mid-1970's several cases in New York, Texas, and elsewhere were brought before the Supreme Court. The court ruled that children were entitled to a bilingual education. They would be taught in Spanish and English, so they would have equal opportunity to learn.

As a result, in many parts of the country signs are posted in Spanish and English. Forms and applications appear in both languages. Children learn in their native tongue and their new one.

However, a report issued in 1984 shows that Hispanics have the highest overall school dropout rate in the nation— 19 percent. The report indicates that Hispanics who remain in school have poor test scores and are not being well educated. One reason, researchers say, may be because schools Hispanics attend are usually overcrowded and poorly equipped.

Some Americans do not approve of the trend toward bilingualism in this country. They point out that every immigrant group that has come to America has had to learn English to get along. They feel Hispanics should not get special treatment, but should learn to read, write, and speak English.

## AMERICAN INDIANS

A beautifully decorated, flared jar with intricate designs made by a Pueblo Indian rests in a museum display case near a beaded and befeathered headdress once worn by a Blackfoot Indian chief. The faded colors of a totem pole speak of mystery and myth. Signs tell hushed visitors about the Indian way of life.

Indians originally migrated to North America thousands of years ago. Over time, Indians developed rich cultures. They created art and artifacts, such as pottery, skillfully woven blankets, and baskets. Each of the many tribes had developed its own myths, stories, and way of life. One strong belief Indian tribes shared was the necessity of living in harmony with nature. But the history of European Americans and American Indians is one of conflicts, broken treaties, and misunderstandings.

By the 1890s, Indians had been deprived of their land and sent to live on reservations. At this time, attempts were made to "Americanize" Indians by educating them to accept American clothes, life-styles, ideas, and beliefs. In the process of influencing the Indians, their own culture, beliefs, and heritage were greatly neglected.

The rights of Indians were not of concern to many Americans. Indians were not granted full citizenship until after 1924.

Indians struggled for years with problems of poverty, dis-

ease, bad housing, and poor medical care. Despite these hardships, the Indian population increased from a low of 300,000 to about 800,000 in 1960. At the same time, more and more Indians realized they were being treated unfairly and unequally. Encouraged by the civil-rights movement, Indian activists began to make demands for their rights.

One of the most famous incidents was the seizure of Alcatraz, a former federal prison and island in San Francisco Bay, in November 1969. By the end of the month, more than 600 Indians from fifty different tribes were living on Alcatraz Island.

One reason the Indians seized Alcatraz was to demonstrate that in its abandoned state, life in the prison was remarkably like life on the reservations—without adequate health care, education, and employment opportunities—difficult, depressing, and hard. Eventually federal authorities removed the Indians, but the tribes had made their point. American Indians wanted a share in equal rights with the rest of the nation.

Today, after decades of battles with government agencies, things are improving for some Indians. The White Mountain Apaches, living in Arizona, have created a successful ski resort with money from a federal grant, as well as a prospering timber company.

*Six months after taking possession of Alcatraz Island, American Indians held a Liberation Day ceremony. Although federal authorities later regained control of the island, the Indians succeeded in dramatizing their struggle for equality.*

But many Indians are still struggling with problems of poverty and high unemployment. Like members of other minorities, they often live in a world that is outside the mainstream of American culture.

American Indians want to learn a way of taking part in American culture. But whether they are successful, or still fighting battles with poverty, they do not want to merge at the expense of losing their own heritage and identity.

## THE HANDICAPPED

Discrimination may be subtle or blatant; it may be difficult to detect or very obvious. Throughout the last several years, more and more people have become aware of the impact discrimination has on themselves and others. Discrimination often results in inequality. For example, some studies show that people who are shorter or heavier than the average may receive fewer employment opportunities—including promotions and raises—than those who are not. It may be difficult for a person to know whether his or her employer is discriminating consciously or unconsciously, that is, intentionally or without realizing it. Sometimes an employer might claim to be unprejudiced and fair, and yet ignore the needs of a particular minority group. One such group includes the handicapped—men, women, and children with physical disabilities.

The handicapped form one of the largest minorities in America. There are estimates that one out of six individuals suffers from some kind of serious physical problem. Disabilities can affect people of any age, income, or race. Some people are born with disabilities, others acquire them through accident or disease.

*Making schools, public buildings, and
business offices accessible to the physically
challenged enables them to be independent,
contributing members of society.*

There is a wide range of disabilities that can afflict a person. Some of the handicapped are partly or completely blind or deaf. Some have difficulty speaking or may be mute—unable to speak at all. Some have trouble using their arms, hands, legs, or feet, or may have lost one or more limbs. Many of these disabilities can complicate daily life.

A child in a wheelchair, for example, might have trouble getting on a school bus or navigating the halls that lead to the classrooms or cafeteria. The child may not be able to maneuver the chair up steps to go to the library, or down the aisles of movie theaters, or among the crowded tables in a restaurant. Trouble and complications can arise just about anywhere—anywhere most people can walk.

Some authors note that for years people tended to treat the handicapped, regardless of their age or abilities, as though they were inferiors or children. Opportunities for the disabled to have physical access to buildings, schools, jobs, or recreational facilities were severely limited and often nonexistent. As a result, discrimination was rampant.

Over the years, laws, attitudes, and practices have changed. Schools, universities, and businesses have begun to provide additional services to assist the handicapped. Special parking spaces for the disabled are placed close to stores, banks, and libraries to make these places more accessible. Ramps and walkways enable those on crutches or wheelchair-bound to enter buildings more easily. Elevator buttons are frequently coded in braille, the system of dots that enables the blind to read. Special equipment allows the handicapped to enjoy using pools, gymnasiums, and other recreational areas. Many handicapped people are eager to demonstrate that with a little mechanical or personal assistance, they can contribute to the society they live in as useful, independent, and resourceful citizens.

# THE ELDERLY

In 1975, it was estimated that one out of ten people in the United States was sixty-five or older; by the year 2025, that number will increase to one out of six. The elderly often find themselves in the same position as other minority groups— they are frequently poor, unwanted, depressed, and often discriminated against.

One problem arises as a result of society's attitudes toward the aged. Our culture idealizes youth and the appearance of youthfulness and beauty. Advertisements offer creams, beauty aids, hair dye, and surgery as remedies to guard against the aging process. Movies and television programs portray glamorous young people in active roles enjoying life. As their bodies age, many men and women find themselves being rejected by others. Yet because of advances in medicine, nutrition, and health care, people are living longer. Older men and women want to remain productive.

One area of particular concern for older Americans is retirement. For many years, companies had policies that required men and women to retire at age sixty-five. Some companies are reversing this trend; and some individuals are bringing lawsuits against agencies and employers that still have mandatory retirement ages. Many people feel they would like to continue to work as long as they are able to do so. They want the economic, intellectual, and financial rewards and independence that working brings.

All Americans want equal rights. From each of these special groups—Hispanics, American Indians, the handicapped, and the elderly—as well as other minorities, we can learn to accept variations from the average in physical appearance, personal beliefs, and cultural practices. We may look different, be old or young, white or black, healthy or ill. But we all want and deserve our rights. We are alike in our common needs, desires, hopes, and dreams. We are alike in our common humanity. In that humanity, we are, each and every one, the same. It is this sameness we must all learn to recognize.

# ★ 8 ★

## WORKING
## TOWARD
## EQUALITY

Many scholars, politicians, and citizens believe that in a democracy, economic rights are as important as civil and political rights. The federal government has responded to that belief by enacting laws and making policies aimed at promoting economic equality and fulfilling the needs of its people.

Many of these plans have generated enormous controversy. And whether they agree or disagree with a specific public policy, most people wonder how far should government go? How much help is too much?

## AFFIRMATIVE ACTION

In order to counteract past discrimination, the U.S. government instituted a policy known as affirmative action. The goal of this plan was to increase the number of women and minority members in the work force.

Those who are against affirmative action often believe that it is wrong or impossible to correct past discrimination by favoring minorities and women. Because of discrimination, these minority groups were often unable to get jobs or, having secured positions, were frequently passed over for promotions or raises. Opponents of the policy say that as a result of affirmative action, a new kind of reverse discrimination occurs. In other words, they believe that blacks, women, and members of other minorities are sometimes favored only because of their minority status, just as white males were once favored because of being white males. When reverse discrimination comes into play, white males are the victims. Opponents of affirmative action feel jobs and promotions should be given to the best candidate regardless of his or her status.

People who agree with the practice of affirmative action often believe, too, that ideally jobs should be given regardless of status. But they point out that without affirmative action, many qualified women and minority candidates face discrimination. They cite experience to support their arguments. Until businesses were forced to do so, they rarely hired women and minority members or promoted them to high-ranking positions. Those who favor affirmative action believe that many employers are prejudiced, either consciously or unconsciously. Without affirmative action, they believe, jobs and educational opportunities would not be given to deserving women and minority members.

## EDUCATION AND
## EQUAL OPPORTUNITY

Many people, including politicians and lawmakers, believe that a good education is the key to getting better jobs—and ultimately a higher standard of living. They say that because of poor education, discrimination, and other factors, many people have not been able to better their life-styles. They believe a good education is the remedy. They claim that those people who will take advantage of it would naturally succeed, because our society rewards hard-working, motivated people. They are in favor of educational reforms and improvements rather than so-called "free rides" or government "charity." Success, they say, must be earned.

In contrast, many experts believe that education alone is not the solution to enable people to get ahead. They say education is good in itself, but should not be considered the best way to create economic equality. Some studies have shown that past a certain point, there is no cause and effect link between education and higher income. These people believe that more government intervention is needed to provide jobs, housing, medical care, and other necessities in order to achieve greater economic equality.

## ECONOMIC ASSISTANCE

In order to promote greater economic equality in America, the government has launched numerous programs to assist the poor or needy. Some of these include programs such as Social Security, which provides income for retired or disabled people and their families; various health-care programs to assist people to receive medical attention or to pay bills for the care they receive; aid to help families to pay rent and provide necessities; food-stamp programs, which enable people to purchase food and household staples. Most of these programs, and many others, are designed to help people who would otherwise sink into poverty.

Some Americans believe that government intervention to help people is crucial—that if life, liberty, and the pursuit of ppiness are the democratic rights of every citizen, then life's necessities such as shelter, food, money, and other commodities needed to preserve life are rights as well.

Other citizens believe limited assistance to solve the problems of the poor and promote economic equality is the answer. Many Americans believe that if too much governmental assistance is given, motivation to succeed through hard work is killed.

## WORKING TOWARD EQUALITY

In order to understand the present state of equality, and more important its future, it is essential to understand the past. As we have seen, the idea of equality has undergone many changes in the course of history. Equality has meant different things to those who lived in medieval England, colonial America, to women at the turn of the twentieth century, to blacks and other minorities in the 1960s—in short to all Americans.

In striving for equality, people have tried to eliminate its opposites—all the barriers that stood in the way and prevented them from fulfilling their dreams, hopes, and ideals. That is why defeating segregation, discrimination, prejudice, tyranny, slavery, and other social evils has so much importance. It is why people sought equality during the American Revolution, the Civil War, and the American civil-rights movement.

Equality has an impact on every aspect of people's lives. It determines their rights as citizens, their economic opportunities, where they live, work, play, go to school, how they will be treated by the rest of the society they live in. That is one of the reasons equality has always been something more than an abstract idea—it is a reality that people have believed in passionately and struggled and sometimes died for.

Because we are all human, we all deserve equal rights. We deserve to be permitted to practice our customs, beliefs, ideals, insofar as they do not interfere with the rights of others. In order to achieve equality, we must recognize these rights.

The future of equality depends on us as individuals and as members of society. We can always make the choice not to discriminate, not to feel prejudice or bigotry toward others. We can encourage others to treat each individual as an individual, as a person in his or her own right. We can encourage people to extend equal rights to all who seek them—not just to a few select groups.

In order to assure a place for equality, we must recognize that although we are individuals with different talents and abilities, we have all been truly "created equal." We have similar needs, feelings, dreams, ideals. From the earliest man and woman who ever lived, to those of the present, to those who will someday populate our planet, we have all shared the capacity for love, laughter, joy, sorrow—for life. Equality is the right of every human, because of the very simple fact that he or she is human.

★★★★

# INDEX